AF583783

DUDE.
BE NICE

DUDE. BE NICE

WRITTEN BY SARAH SCHEERGER WITH BRENT & JAMIE CAMALICH
ILLUSTRATED BY ALEX MACNAUGHTON

SCHOLASTIC

Scholastic Australia
PO Box 579 Gosford NSW 2250
ABN 11 000 614 577
www.scholastic.com.au

Part of the Scholastic Group
Sydney • Auckland • New York • Toronto • London • Mexico City
• New Delhi • Hong Kong • Buenos Aires • Puerto Rico

Published by Scholastic Australia in 2026.

Published by arrangement with Flamingo Books, an imprint of Penguin Young Readers Group, a division of Penguin Random House LLC.

ISBN 978-1-76172-876-1

Printed in China by RR Donnelley.

Scholastic Australia's policy, in association with RR Donnelley, is to use papers that are renewable and made efficiently with wood from responsibly managed sources, so as to minimise its environmental footprint.

10 9 8 7 6 5 4 3 2 1 26 27 28 29 30 / 2

To the dedicated folks working in schools,
spreading kindness. We see you out there,
making a difference and changing lives.
—S. S., J. C. & B. C.

To Rosie, for all your support and
the cups of tea
—A. M.

Meet Dude.

Dude's a nice dude.

(Most of the time.)

He says "please"
and "thank you,"

he picks up trash,

and he's always cheerful.

One morning, Dude has an idea.

"Today I'm going to be **EXTRA** nice," Dude decides.

"In fact, I'll do **EVERYTHING** nice **ALL** day long."

"Look! I even made a plan," Dude proclaims.
"It's an excellent plan."
Fizz knows all about Dude and his plans.
"I'd better help," she worries.
But Dude doesn't hear . . .

MY
EXCELLENT PLAN

- Free some bees.
- Pick pesky lint.
- Hug a porcupine.
- Water the weeds.
- Comb a cat.
- Floss someone's hard-to-reach places.
- Bathe a bug.
- Sing in someone's ear.

He's out to be nice, and nice he'll be.

"Hey, WAIT! What's that? Is it lint?
Stuck all over that sweater?
Nobody likes lint all over their sweater."
Aha! Dude knows *just* how to help.
"Picking lint is a pesky job," Dude decides.
"I'll help with that!"

Fizz waddles along, trying to catch up.
"Do you want some tweezers?
Pliers? A toothpick? To borrow my beak?"
But Dude doesn't hear. He's far too busy being nice.

"There. That was nice of me,"
Dude decides.

Fizz hurries after him.
"Um, Dude?" she asks.
But Dude doesn't hear.

Dude sees his friend. "Is that melty ice cream? Dripping down a crunchy cone?" Dude asks. Aha! He knows *just* how to help.

Fizz dances over to Dude. "Ooh, ooh, can I help with that too?"

"There. That was nice of me," Dude decides.

Fizz hurries after him.

"Um, Dude?" she asks.

But Dude doesn't hear.

He's far too busy being nice.

"Look, Fizz, those poor puppies need a walk."
Dude hurries ahead. "I'll help with that!"
Dude's out to be nice, and nice he'll be.

"There. That was nice of me," Dude decides as he untangles himself. "Being extra nice feels extra good. How else can I help?"

Dude looks under.

Dude looks over.

Dude sees a party nearby.

"Are those flames? On that CAKE?"

Aha! Dude knows *just* how to help.

"Stand back. I'll help with that!"

"Dude, wait!" Fizz cries. "Those are . . . "

". . . birthday candles on a birthday cake.

A WET birthday cake."

"There. That was nice of me," Dude decides.
"Oh, I have an idea. This will be EXTRA nice.
Here, Fizz. I know you love blue."
"Dude?" Fizz squeaks, beginning to float.
But Dude doesn't hear.
He's far too busy being nice.

Dude's out to be nice, and nice he'll be, when . . .

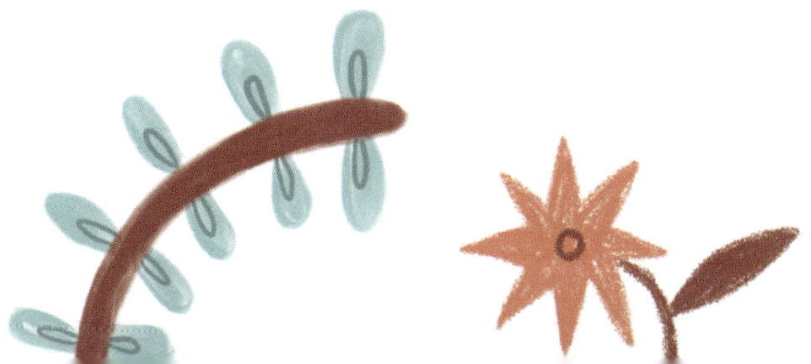

Splat! Dude falls flat.
He peels himself off the ground,
his eyes wide.
Someone made a slippery mess.
And he has a sneaking suspicion
that someone was HIM.

Dude feels terrible. "I had a plan, an excellent plan," he says in a teeny-tiny voice. "I was just trying to be nice."

Just then, Fizz cries, "Duuuuuuuude . . ."

But Dude doesn't hear.

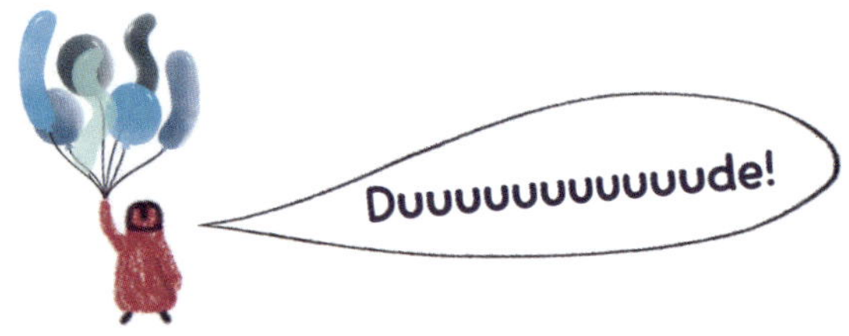

Fizz cries again, "Duuuuuuuuuuuuuuuuuuuuuuuuuuuuuuuuuuude . . ."

Dude spies a tiny speck high in the sky.

"Fizz, what are you doing way up there?

Do you need help?"

"YEEEEESSSSSSS," Fizz cries from far, far away.

Dude wants to help.

But Fizz is too far, too high, and too tiny up there in the sky. Besides, Dude doesn't have enough arms. And there's simply no time to grow more.

Dude needs a new plan.

"Fizz is in trouble," Dude calls out.
"We need a team, a Terrific Team!
Who wants to help?"
One by one by one,
the others volunteer.

I'll help with that!

Let's make a new plan, an excellent plan!

We like to help!

Thanks for asking!

Sure!

They stack friend on top of friend on top of friend . . . until they reach Fizz.

"Thanks, everyone. That was nice of us," Dude decides. "I've been thinking . . . Maybe being extra nice sometimes means asking for extra help?"

Dude looks all around.
"Someone should clean up this mess.
Oh, wait! What if *we* help with that?"
"I do like to help," Fizz says softly.
"But should we ask if they WANT help?"
"ASK?" Dude considers this for the very first time.
"Yes, asking is nice," he agrees.

Can we help
with that?
Sure!
Can we help
with that?
Most
definitely.

"There, we cleaned up nicely,"
the Terrific Team decides with high fives.
"Cleaning up is definitely nice," they all agree.

MY pretty good
~~EXCELLENT~~ PLAN
Offer to help.
· Ask first.
· Listen.
· Let friends help too.
· Ask before hugging.
Take turns on the
ampoline.
errific team.
w friends.
dog at a time.
parties.
nds warm.
resents.

Fizz looks left. She looks right. "Dude's a nice dude," Fizz muses. "He's been trying to be EXTRA nice ALL day long. That's why I have an EXTRA-nice surprise for him."

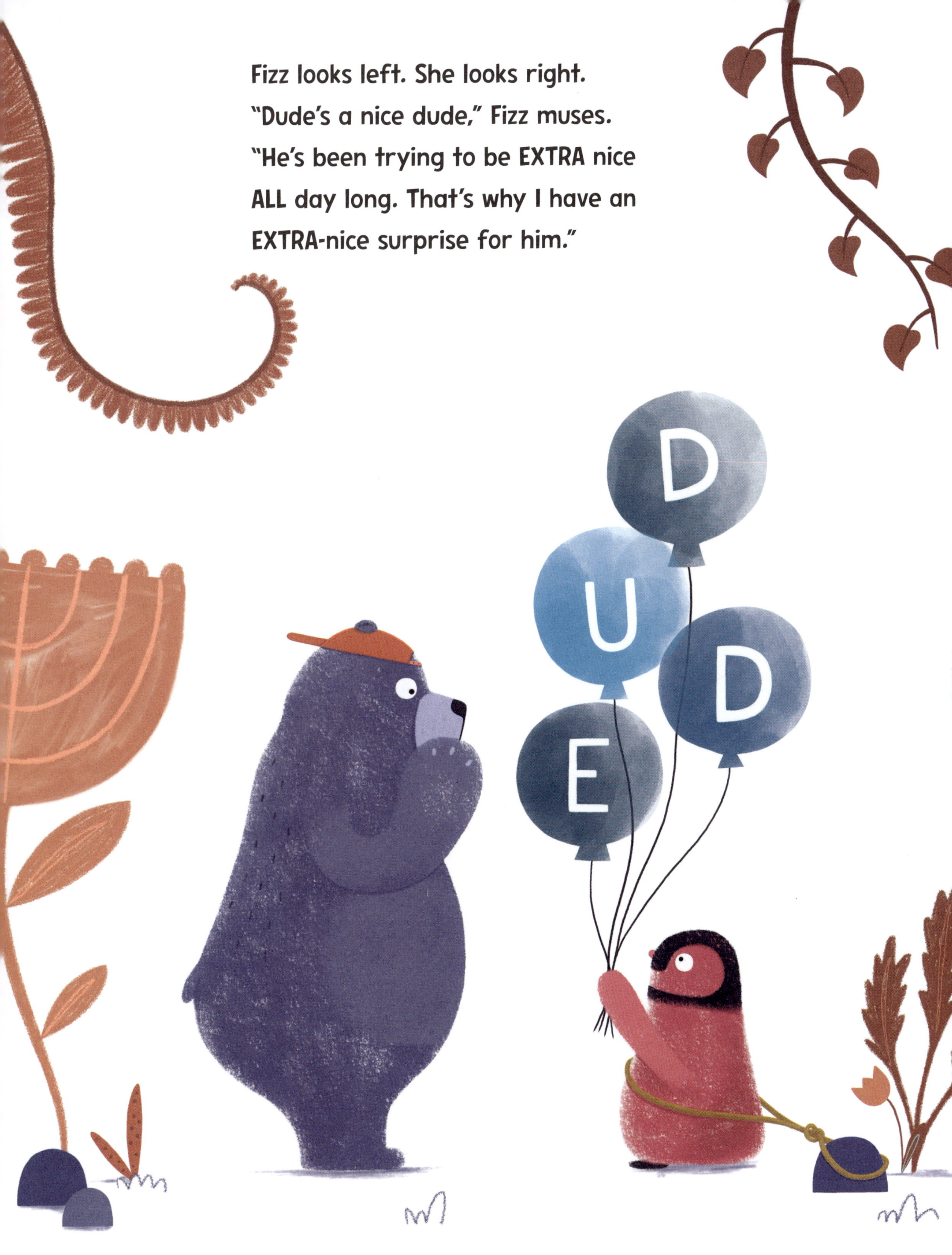

"There." Fizz waddles away.
"That was nice of me."